DRONES ARE EVERYWHERE!

DRONES
FOR RACING
AND SPORTS

BARBARA M. LINDE

PowerKiDS
press™

New York

Thanks to Michael A. Roy, research assistant.

Published in 2020 by The Rosen Publishing Group, Inc.
29 East 21st Street, New York, NY 10010

First Edition

Editor: Shannon Harts
Book Design: Tanya Dellaccio

Photo Credits: Cover (background) NCS Production/Shutterstock.com; cover (drone) BorneoJC James/Shutterstock.com; series background Djem/Shuttertock.com; p. 5 eddystocker/Shutterstock.com; p. 6 AFP/Getty Images; p. 7 goodluz/Shutterstock.com; p. 9 Felix Mizioznikov/Shutterstock.com; p. 11 (main) JUNG YEON-JE/AFP/Getty Images; p. 11 (inset) Alexander Hassenstein/Getty Images Sport/Getty Images; p. 12 Jonathan Bachman/Getty Images Sports/Getty Images; p. 13 Pool/Getty Images Sport/Getty Images; p. 15 Luis Lamar/National Geographic Image Collection/Getty Images; p. 16 picture alliance/Getty Images; p. 17 Bloomberg/Getty Images; p. 19 Steve Paston/PA Images/Getty Images; p. 21 asiseeit/E+/Getty Images; p. 22 Bruce Bennett/Getty Images News/Getty Images.

Cataloging-in-Publication Data

Names: Linde, Barbara M.
Title: Drones for racing and sports / Barbara M. Linde.
Description: New York : PowerKids Press, 2020. | Series: Drones are everywhere! | Includes glossary and index.
Identifiers: ISBN 9781725309302 (pbk.) | ISBN 9781725309326 (library bound) | ISBN 9781725309319 (6 pack)
Subjects: LCSH: Drone aircraft–Juvenile literature. | Sports–Technological innovations–Juvenile literature.
Classification: LCC TL685.35 L56 2020 | DDC 797.5'2–dc23

Manufactured in the United States of America

CPSIA Compliance Information: Batch #CWPK20. For Further Information contact Rosen Publishing, New York, New York at 1-800-237-9932.

CONTENTS

IT'S A DRONE!

You hear a loud buzzing sound. You look in the sky. Something is flying up high and then it zips down low. You may think it looks like a big bug with several arms. But there's a spinning **propeller** on top of each arm. There aren't any wires or wings. It's too small for a person to fit inside.

What is this thing? It's a drone. How are drones used in racing and in sports? Keep reading to find out.

DRONE DETAILS

MANY PEOPLE DON'T LIKE THE SOUND OF DRONES. THE BUZZING NOISE SCARES SOME PEOPLE. A STUDY FOUND THAT THE SOUND ANNOYS, OR BOTHERS, PEOPLE MORE THAN THE SOUND OF CARS OR TRUCKS.

Many drones fly low enough that it's easy to see and hear them. Personal drones must fly at or below 400 feet (122 m) at all times, according to U.S. government rules in 2019.

THE PARTS OF A DRONE

The parts that make the drone run are mainly found in its body. A part called the landing gear helps the drone land smoothly. A **GPS** can tell the drone where to fly. On a common kind of drone called a quadcopter, there are four "arms." A **motor** in each arm powered by **batteries** spins propellers that lift the drone.

Most drones have a camera that lets the person using the drone see what the drone sees. A **pilot** on the ground directs the drone using a controller or a smartphone.

DRONE DETAILS

SOME DRONES ARE MADE OF PLASTIC. OTHERS ARE MADE OF MATERIAL, OR MATTER, THAT IS EVEN LIGHTER THAN PLASTIC, SUCH AS CARBON FIBER.

To become a drone pilot, you must be at least 16 years old according to U.S. government rules in 2019.

WATCHING SPORTS ON TV

Have you watched a sports game on TV? Did you feel like a bird flying above the field? When you looked down, you could likely see everything. Then you flew in close and got near each player.

A drone with a camera likely **filmed** the game. A sports field might also have cameras on wires or poles. These can't move beyond the wires or poles and may not get the best shots. Drones can move in all directions, so they can get closer to the action and get better shots.

DRONE DETAILS

IN 2018, A MAN FELL OFF A CLIFF WHILE CLIMBING A TALL MOUNTAIN IN THE HIMALAYAS, A MOUNTAIN RANGE IN ASIA. MANY THOUGHT HE WAS DEAD. LUCKILY, A DRONE FOUND HIM, AND PEOPLE CAME TO SAVE HIM.

The U.S. government does not allow personal drones to fly over sporting events one hour before and after the event.

THE WINTER OLYMPIC GAMES

Drones helped out at the 2014 Winter **Olympic Games**. They filmed the **skiers** zipping down hills. Drones also got great shots of flipping **snowboarders**. This was the first time drones were widely used at the Olympics.

The 2018 Olympics started with a special show. For those watching it on TV, about 1,200 drones lit up the sky! They formed the Olympic Rings, a snowboarder, and a bird. Every night, when the winners received their prizes, there were often drone shows at those events, too. Another show ended the games.

DRONE DETAILS

10 DURING THE 2018 OLYMPICS, SPECIAL DRONES WERE USED TO HELP KEEP PEOPLE SAFE BY CATCHING DRONES THAT COULD BE HARMFUL.

The 2018 Olympics opening show set a record for the largest number of drones ever used at one time!

11

PRACTICE, PRACTICE!

Drones can film whole games. They often take pictures from many angles. Coaches who train players watch the games later—the good and bad plays—to learn how to help their team.

Players film their own practices using drones. Drones allow players to see how they stand, run, and move. They can then make changes and film again. Some **tennis** players use a special drone that drops balls from up high while moving all over the court. The players try to hit the balls so their swings can improve.

DRONE DETAILS

NBA PLAYER AARON GORDON USED A DRONE TO HELP WITH A SLAM DUNK DURING THE 2017 VERIZON SLAM DUNK CONTEST.

The company Intel created the drone that helped with a slam dunk in 2017.

13

GONE FISHING!

Fishing is a big sport for many people. It can be hard to find fish when you are sitting in a boat. To help, a fisher can send up a drone with a camera that shows where the fish are. The fish can't see the drone, so they usually don't get scared away.

Fishers can also see how the fish move and where they hide. They can learn how fish take the **bait**, too. Is there a fish predator nearby? Fishers can watch what the fish do.

DRONE DETAILS

SOME FISHERS SAY THAT THE NOISE OF THE DRONES DOESN'T BOTHER THE FISH.

Drones with cameras can also show fishers how deep the water is and if there are rocks or other things in the water.

DRONE RACING

Drone racing is now a real sport! There are races all over the world. Pilots wear special **goggles** so they can see what the drone sees and feel like they're in the drone—this is called first-person view (FPV). Racing drones follow a set course. There are often twists and turns. There are dips and dives. Drones race around things that are in their way.

Some racing drones can go more than 90 miles (145 km) per hour. You can watch some races on TV and online.

DRONE DETAILS

PILOTS PRACTICE IN THE OPEN AND ON WEBSITES. SOME SAY THEY PRACTICE FOR HOURS EACH DAY!

There are many types of FPV goggles. It's important to make sure find the right fit for you.

PLACES FOR RACES

For many races, not only do the pilots wear the special goggles—so do the watchers. Some courses are in the woods. The drones race one at a time to see who can get the fastest time. Parts of the course are sometimes narrow. It's a tight fit between trees. There are climbs up big hills.

Parks are good places for group races. There's a lot of space, so many drones can race at the same time. Large, unused buildings also make good courses. Drones may fly between boxes and under tables.

DRONE DETAILS

IN 2019, INDIA HELD ITS FIRST DRONE OLYMPICS. DRONES HAD TO CARRY AND DROP A WEIGHT AMONG OTHER COMPETITIONS, OR MATCHES. THEY ALSO HAD TO FLY TOGETHER IN A GROUP. WINNERS GOT UP TO ABOUT $7,000.

Pilots like to show their skills at moving the drones through courses during races.

FIXING PROBLEMS

When using drones for racing or other sports, you may run into some common problems—but there's often an easy fix. Is the battery not lasting? You could try buying a stronger one. If the drone isn't flying evenly, a propeller might be bent and you could try fixing it by bending it back into place.

If the motor is getting too hot, some parts of the motor probably need to be switched out. Finally, if you're using goggles and the FPV video isn't working, try moving away from other drones or fixing the controller.

Sometimes, you'll be able to fix your drone yourself. Other times, you might need help from an adult.

WHAT COMES NEXT?

Using drones to film sporting events has been a big success. In the coming years, you may see more of it. Some new drones will likely be able to get closer to the players. They may even be able to stay over a player for a whole game.

New drones will also be smarter. They'll do more without a pilot, such as moving away from objects that get too close. They'll also get faster and stronger, too. As more companies make drones, they'll likely get less expensive and more people will use them for racing and sports.

GLOSSARY

bait: Something, such as food, that is used to attract an animal, such as a fish, so they can be caught.

battery: A device placed inside a machine, such as a flashlight, to supply it with electricity.

film: To record something with a video camera.

goggles: Special glasses that guard the eyes.

GPS: An abbreviation for global positioning system. A device that uses satellite signals to tell people or machines where they are, and to provide directions to other locations.

motor: A machine that produces motion or power for doing work.

Olympic Games: An international sports competition held once every 2 years, alternating between summer and winter games.

pilot: Someone who flies an aircraft.

propeller: Paddle-like parts on an aircraft that spin to move the plane forward in addition to up and down.

skier: A person who moves over snow on two long, narrow boards attached to their feet.

snowboarder: A person who moves over snow on one board.

tennis: A game where two or four players use rackets to hit a ball over a net on a court.

INDEX

WEBSITES

Due to the changing nature of Internet links, PowerKids Press has developed an online list of websites related to the subject of this book. This site is updated regularly. Please use this link to access the list: www.powerkidslinks.com/dae/racing